A Tale of Two Poggles

Written by Margi McAllister

Illustrated by Mark Beech

UPPER POGGLE   Nether Poggle

ISBN-13: 978-0-328-83297-2
ISBN-10: 0-328-83297-9
2 3 4 5 6 7 8 9 10 V0B4 19 18 17 16 15

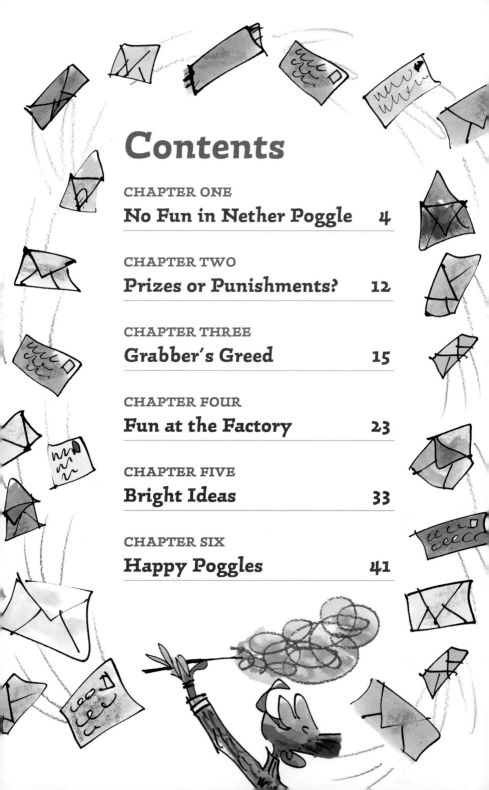

Contents

CHAPTER ONE

No Fun in Nether Poggle

Once there was a small town called Nether Poggle, and I wish I could tell you that it was a lovely place to live, but it wasn't. Most Nether Poggle people were bored or sad or both, and this is why.

In the middle of the town was a factory called Grabber's Envelopes. All day, every day, Grabber's made envelopes—brown, gray, and white ones, from the largest to the tiniest and all sizes in between. They made nothing else, only envelopes, and thousands of envelopes were made in that factory every week and sent away to the shops. The factory was long and gray and looked a bit like an envelope itself.

Most of the adults in Nether Poggle worked at Grabber's Envelopes. They didn't like it there because the work was boring, the factory was cold, and they didn't get paid very much. But there weren't many other places to work nearby. There was no train station in Nether Poggle, and not even a bus stop, so people in Nether Poggle were stuck.

There was one person in Nether Poggle who could have made the whole town much, much happier. Her name was Gloria Grabber, and she was the Mayoress of Nether Poggle, which made her very important. She had the power to decide what happened in the town. Gloria Grabber was tall and thin and always very beautifully dressed. She owned the envelope factory. If you ever wanted to do anything new or different in Nether Poggle, you had to ask her first.

7

Gloria Grabber hated the Internet more than anything, and Nether Poggle did not have access to the Internet because she wouldn't allow it. She hated cell phones too, so there were no cell phone towers near Nether Poggle, which meant cell phones didn't work there. She said that nobody should send e-mails or text messages. They should write letters by hand, put them in envelopes, and mail them. In Nether Poggle, even postcards had to be sent in envelopes! When Nether Poggle School sent letters home to the children's parents, every single page had to be in its own individual envelope. Gloria Grabber made the rules, and what she loved most was money, and envelopes. She had *always* made money by selling envelopes.

One wet morning in February, Gloria Grabber
went to Nether Poggle School to talk to the children
at an assembly. She looked very sternly down at them
and talked for much too long about the importance
of good handwriting, hard work, and putting letters in
envelopes; but not all the children were listening.

Alejandro and Nina certainly weren't listening.
Alejandro was daydreaming about what he wanted to
be when he grew up.

I could be an astronaut, he thought, as Gloria Grabber
went on talking, *or a pilot, or a train conductor. Either way
I definitely don't want to work in an envelope factory.*

Nina was thinking about what she wanted to be when she grew up too. She wondered about being an engineer, or an inventor, or a game designer. *I want to make things work,* she thought. *Whatever I do, I know I don't want to work in an envelope factory.*

"And finally," said Gloria Grabber, "your teachers have told me that today they want you to write a story about what you would like to be when you grow up."

Nina's and Alejandro's eyes suddenly lit up, and they started listening.

"You might want to be like me and have your own factory," she said. "Or you might like to come and work for me!"

Alejandro and Nina groaned very, very quietly.

"So off you go, children, and write your lovely stories," said Gloria Grabber, "and I will give a wonderful prize for the very best ones!"

CHAPTER TWO

Prizes or Punishments?

That evening, Alejandro sat at the kitchen table and wrote a long story all about flying and driving, and about going into space! He wrote about driving trains up and down hills and through tunnels. Nina went home and wrote all about the wonderful machines she wanted to make. Machines that whirled, rolled, whizzed, and shone.

The next week, Gloria Grabber came to school to talk to the children again.

"I've read all your lovely, exciting stories," she said, "and many of you chose to write about how much you would like to work in my factory." She paused. "But I think the very *best* stories were written by Alejandro Mendez and Nina Penn."

Everyone cheered and clapped, while Alejandro and Nina looked at each other with surprise. Gloria Grabber gave a sneaky smile.

"And I have such a wonderful prize for you!" said Gloria, with a knowing look.

Alejandro and Nina wondered what the prize would be. Would it be a visit to an amusement park? Or a gift card for their favorite bookstore in Upper Poggle? Even a *trip* to Upper Poggle would be good.

"The prize," said Gloria, her smile widening, "is to spend a whole day visiting my factory!"

"Thank you very much," said Alejandro and Nina, realizing now why *they* had won the prize. They tried to sound polite, but they were very disappointed.

Gloria Grabber frowned at them and gave a scornful look.

"I am the Lady Mayoress," she said. "You may call me 'Madam Mayoress.'"

"Yes, Madam Mayoress," said Alejandro and Nina. But it didn't matter what they called her, it was still a really rotten prize.

"Never mind," said Nina to Alejandro later. "I guess we'll see what our moms and dads do all day."

"Oh, yes," grumbled Alejandro, "sorting envelopes. That'll be fun."

CHAPTER THREE
Grabber's Greed

The nearest town to Nether Poggle was Upper Poggle, and Upper Poggle was completely different from Nether Poggle! It was a modern, exciting town with lots of shops and modern cafés. The cafés had wireless connection, so people could go to drink hot chocolate, meet friends, and use the Internet. It had a movie theater, a mall, a sports arena, a swimming pool, and lots of parks and green spaces. The only thing Upper Poggle didn't have was a parking lot.

Upper Poggle

The next Monday morning, Alejandro and Nina walked to the factory together with their parents. It was a cold, wet, and windy day, and Nina pulled her coat tightly around herself to keep warm.

"If only we could go to Upper Poggle," she grumbled. "It's much more fun there."

"I'm going to try to save up my money," said Alejandro. "Then I might be able to move to Upper Poggle when I grow up."

The workers all went into the factory looking bored and miserable, their heads hung low. Once they got inside, Alejandro and Nina weren't surprised that people were so miserable. The factory looked even grimmer inside than it did on the outside. All the walls were gray, and the paint was peeling. There was no carpet on the floor, and there were no chairs to sit on. Some of the workers climbed the stairs to a mezzanine that ran all the way around the room. At one end of the floor were two spinning disks divided into sections, which looked rather like carousels.

Everybody looked up automatically when Gloria Grabber strode in, her high heels *click-clacking* on the bare floor. Nobody liked her. She was wearing a bright red dress and her Mayoress's gold chain around her neck, so at least she looked colorful.

"Listen up!" she called to the workers. "Before you start work today, I have some very important announcements to make. First, we have Alejandro and Nina here from Nether Poggle School joining us today to see what we do. Now that they're here they may as well help, so somebody give them jobs and show them what to do."

"She's using us as free workers!" whispered Nina.

"Alejandro, Nina," said Gloria, "don't go getting trapped in any machinery. The hospital is a long way away, and I won't be taking you there. So just do as you're told and stay out of everyone's way. Now . . . my other announcement is very, very important."

She paused until everyone was looking at her and then went on.

"I've told you all before that nobody writes letters anymore. It's no good—we're just not selling enough envelopes, and the factory's hardly making any money. So I've decided to sell it."

The workers gasped. Then they all looked at each other and started talking.

Beige envelopes

Brown envelopes

more Brown envelopes

ite elopes Gray

"Somebody might buy it and make it into a café," said Nina, "or a place for inventors to make things. "

"Or a skating rink," said Alejandro, "or something even more fun, like a bowling alley or a movie theater!"

Nina's dad, who worked in the factory, raised his hand.

"Madam Mayoress," he said, "some of us have been saying that we'd like to get together, all the workers, and buy the factory."

"What a great idea!" said Alejandro. "Then we can all decide what to do with it!"

"Certainly not," snapped Gloria Grabber. "I've already arranged to sell it to the Mayor of Upper Poggle, and that is a done deal. They have many visitors coming to the town who look for spaces to park their cars. The factory is to be knocked down. The land will be used for a parking lot, with shuttle buses to take everyone into Upper Poggle."

"But then where will we work, Madam Mayoress?" asked Nina's dad.

Gloria Grabber shrugged. "That is your problem," she said.

"No it isn't, it's yours!" called Nina. Then she remembered that she was only there to visit and wasn't supposed to say anything, but it was too late now. "You're the Mayoress and you're supposed to care about the people in Nether Poggle and make it a good place to live!"

Gloria Grabber clapped her hands. "Right back to work, everyone!" she said. "We've wasted enough time already!" And she glared at Nina. "I don't want another word out of you, all day. Just keep out of the way, both of you!"

All the workers put on thin, white gloves so that they wouldn't get the envelopes dirty. Alejandro and Nina stood on the factory floor and watched while the machinery came to life.

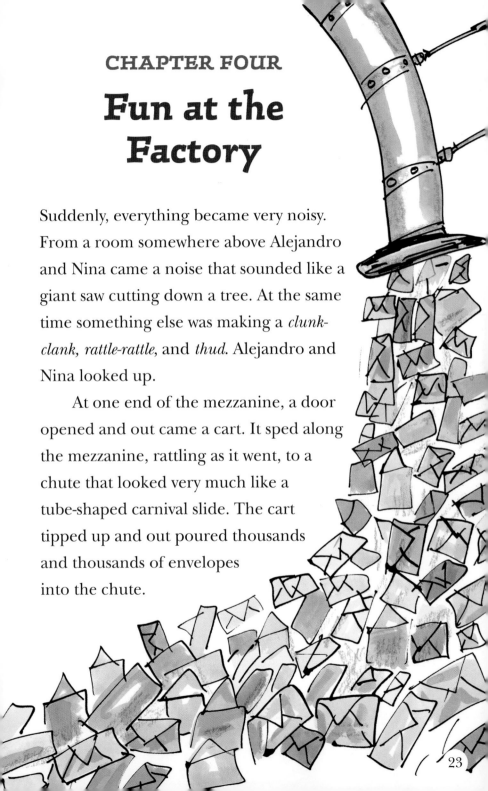

CHAPTER FOUR

Fun at the Factory

Suddenly, everything became very noisy. From a room somewhere above Alejandro and Nina came a noise that sounded like a giant saw cutting down a tree. At the same time something else was making a *clunk-clank, rattle-rattle,* and *thud.* Alejandro and Nina looked up.

At one end of the mezzanine, a door opened and out came a cart. It sped along the mezzanine, rattling as it went, to a chute that looked very much like a tube-shaped carnival slide. The cart tipped up and out poured thousands and thousands of envelopes into the chute.

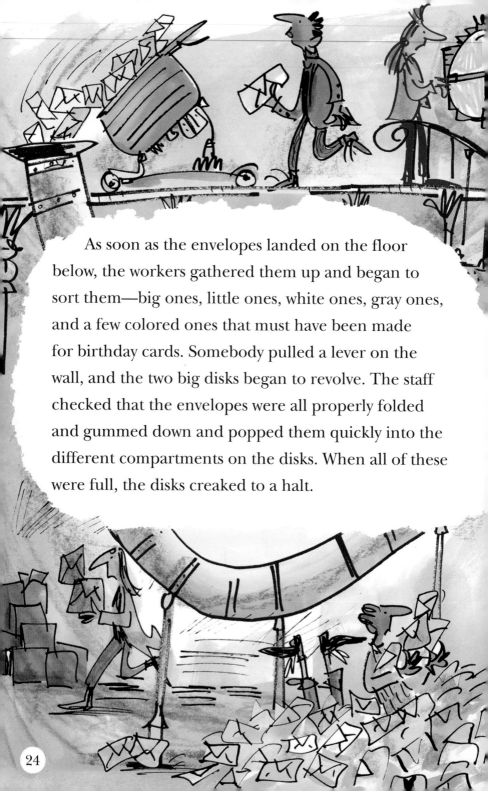

As soon as the envelopes landed on the floor below, the workers gathered them up and began to sort them—big ones, little ones, white ones, gray ones, and a few colored ones that must have been made for birthday cards. Somebody pulled a lever on the wall, and the two big disks began to revolve. The staff checked that the envelopes were all properly folded and gummed down and popped them quickly into the different compartments on the disks. When all of these were full, the disks creaked to a halt.

"Now what?" wondered Nina. They soon found out. Now that the envelopes were sorted, they were packed in boxes and wheeled into another room labeled "Envelope Store." Another load of envelopes flopped down the chute, and then another. The workers were hurrying to keep up with them.

"They'll be up to their knees in envelopes if they slow down!" said Nina.

"Is that what they do all day?" said Alejandro. "It looks so boring!"

Gloria Grabber was *tap-tapping* toward them in her high-heeled shoes. She wheeled a huge cart loaded so high with enormous sheets of paper that Nina could hardly see over it.

"You two!" she yelled. "Take these upstairs!"

"But how . . . " began Nina, staring at the enormous pile of paper.

"Use the elevator!" ordered Gloria, gesturing to an elevator on the other side of the room. Alejandro and Nina found the elevator and wheeled the cart into it. When they reached the upstairs floor, they found out what the sawing noise was. A huge machine was cutting massive sheets of paper into lots of different envelope sizes, while another machine gummed and folded them. Alejandro's mom and dad were on the team packing the finished envelopes into the carts.

"But this is silly!" whispered Alejandro to Nina. "What's the point when they can't even sell the envelopes?"

The same things went on all morning, over and over and over again. Nina saw so many envelopes that she found that she could still see envelopes even when she shut her eyes.

At last a bell rang, and all the workers gave a big sigh of relief and took off their white gloves.

"Lunch time," said one of the workers.

"Thank goodness for that," muttered Alejandro as the doors of the cafeteria opened. It was a lot like the school lunchroom, but smaller, dirtier, and grayer, with bigger tables and less comfortable chairs. Alejandro and Nina soon finished their packed lunches. They wandered back into the factory, which was quiet at last as everyone else was still busy eating lunch.

"Where's Gloria Grabber?" wondered Nina.

"I saw her go out to her car and drive away," said Alejandro, "which means we've got the place to ourselves. All of the machinery is switched off, so how about a ride in one of those carts?"

"We shouldn't!" gasped Nina, but she had to admit that it did sound like fun.

"They're only carts—they don't go fast," said Alejandro. "I think they run on batteries or something, but we don't need to switch them on. One of us could push instead."

"You mean *you* want to ride in the cart, so *I* have to push!" Nina griped.

"We can take turns," said Alejandro as they went up in the elevator to the mezzanine floor.

Nina was beginning to like the idea. Alejandro found a cart and climbed in. Nina pushed it as she ran all the way to the chute. When they reached the chute, Alejandro scrambled out.

"Here I go!" he called, as he hurled himself down the chute and slid onto the pile of envelopes at the other end.

"Fantastic!" he said, picking himself up. "You have to try it!"

They took turns riding in the cart, sliding down the chute, and going back up in the elevator. They were having a wonderful time.

"Let's get the spinning disk things going!" said Alejandro. "This is like an amusement park!"

They pulled the lever and rode on the spinning disks, going around and around and around, until they were dizzy.

Then they wheeled each other around in the carts some more.

"This is what it should be!" called Nina, sliding down the chute for the tenth time. "An amusement park in Nether Poggle!"

Outside, a car door slammed, and they heard the distinctive *click-clacking* of heels.

"Gloria's back!" gasped Nina. "Quick! Hide! She'll be furious!"

CHAPTER FIVE
Bright Ideas

Alejandro and Nina bolted through the nearest door, which was the one marked "Envelope Store." Inside, it was piled high with boxes . . .

and boxes . . .

and boxes . . .

of boring envelopes.

"We're in trouble if she finds us," said Nina, "but it was so much fun!"

"You were right about this place," replied Alejandro. "It should be an amusement park. There are so many things to ride on and slide down! And this room's enormous! It could even have a bowling alley. I'd love a bowling alley."

"Or a hall of mirrors," said Nina, her face cracking a smile as she imagined Gloria being stretched and squeezed. "And there's that other big room upstairs where they cut out the envelopes. That could be anything—you could put a massive ball pit in there for little kids. And then there's space outside where they park the cars for even more fun things!"

"And it would all be painted in bright colors," said Alejandro, "and the cafeteria could sell drinks and snacks."

"And the tables would be different colors," said Nina. Already she was picturing a bright, lively place, full of people whirling on carousels and children rolling around in a ball pit. "And there would be a face-painting booth . . . "

" . . . and a roller coaster!" said Alejandro. "Do you think it could really happen?"

"It could, if enough people wanted it to," said Nina as she opened the door cautiously, just a little, and looked out. "OK, Gloria's gone—we'd better get out of here before anyone comes looking for us."

At snack break in the afternoon, Alejandro and Nina explained their idea to some of the workers.

"Gloria Grabber wants to sell the factory anyway," Nina pointed out. "If she sells it to make a parking lot for Upper Poggle, it just means that more people will go there instead of staying here. So she may as well sell it to us."

"Who do you mean by 'us'?" asked Nina's dad.

"All of us in Nether Poggle!" said Alejandro. "If everyone put some money in, of course."

"I like the idea of an amusement park," said Alejandro's mom. "I'd rather work there than pack envelopes all day."

"So we have to persuade Gloria . . ." began Nina, but then she stopped because the room had become very quiet. All the adults were looking at the door. With all the chit-chat no one had heard Gloria's *click-clacking* as she approached.

Nervously, Alejandro and Nina turned around. Gloria Grabber stood in the doorway, her arms folded and a severe glare on her face.

Alejandro wondered how much Gloria had heard, and Nina felt herself turn pink. She thought only teachers could look at you like that.

"I'd like to speak to you two in my office," Gloria said sternly.

Glancing at each other, Nina and Alejandro followed her into the office. She moved a few boxes of envelopes off her desk and sat down behind it, her elbows on the desk and her fingertips together.

"I heard what you were saying," she began, "and I'd like to know what on earth you were thinking? How *dare* you come in here and tell my workers to buy my factory!"

"But you want to sell it anyway!" said Alejandro.

"I'm selling it to the Mayor of Upper Poggle," replied Gloria, "and that's final."

"Is it?" asked Nina with a sly smile. "Oh, that's a shame. We were talking about something that would bring so much money into the town."

Gloria Grabber had just stood up to open the door, but at the word *money*, she immediately sat down again. Nina gave a small, satisfied smile.

"Tell me more," Gloria ordered.

"Well," explained Alejandro, "this place would make a fantastic amusement park. You see, there's no amusement park in Upper Poggle. People would come here from miles around. They might even come from Upper Poggle!"

"They'd spend lots of money," agreed Nina, "and people here would still have jobs because they could work in the booths and operate the rides and things."

"And you could open the amusement park!" said Alejandro. "And then everyone would say what a good Mayoress you are!"

Nina quietly thought that this was going a bit too far. It was their idea, not Gloria's. But she could also see that Gloria liked the sound of this very, very much.

"Yes," said Gloria thoughtfully, "they would, wouldn't they?"

CHAPTER SIX
Happy Poggles

In very little time the envelope factory was sold to the people of Nether Poggle, who set to work to transform it. They started by painting everything in bright colors. All the envelopes were cleared out, and the envelope store became the bowling alley Alejandro had imagined.

The mezzanine and carts were turned
into roller coaster rides that swooped around
the building! The chute and spinning disks
became a slide and carousel.

Outside, there was a skate park in the summer and a skating rink in the winter, and there was a bouncy castle and a ball pit for little kids. The cafeteria was painted, and new tables and chairs were put in place. It began serving all sorts of food and drink and even cotton candy too! Gloria's office became a gift shop where postcards of Nether Poggle were on sale (but now you didn't have to put them in envelopes).

The amusement park became so popular that busloads of people came to visit it every day. The cafeteria wasn't big enough for them all, so eventually cafés and an ice cream parlor opened in the town too. A new little bakery opened to make bread and cake for the cafés. Soon everyone in Upper and Nether Poggle wanted to shop there.

Nether Poggle got its first-ever bus service, and the local paper, *Post of the Poggles,* ran a whole page about the wonderful Nether Poggle Amusement Park. They interviewed Alejandro and Nina.

"It's a great day out for the whole family," the paper read, "and all because of two clever kids, Alejandro and Nina!"

There was also a picture of Gloria Grabber wearing her red dress and the gold chain, but Nina's and Alejandro's parents knew who had thought of the amusement park first. So did all the people who worked there. And so did—well, so *does*—absolutely everybody in Nether Poggle!

Life worked out well for the people of Nether Poggle, but you may be wondering what happened to Gloria after she sold the factory. Nobody in Nether Poggle wanted her to be the Mayoress any longer, so at the next election, they voted her out.

Soon afterward Gloria drove away in her car, and no one saw her again. The rumor spread in Nether Poggle that she had traveled around the world, spending a lot of money on shoes, jewelry, and staying in very expensive hotels. That was at least until one Friday afternoon when she reappeared in Nether Poggle.

Gloria still hated e-mail and the Internet, but she'd spent all of her money enjoying herself. She had to take the only job she could get, serving in the shop at the amusement park. She still wore the red dress, which was now quite faded, and she still tried to sell envelopes with the postcards . . . but of course no one was interested in envelopes.

And as for the rest of the town, when Gloria was voted out of the election, guess who was elected as Nether Poggle's new Mayor? The people chose Nina's dad. He became a very good Mayor, and if ever he needed good ideas, he just asked Alejandro and Nina.